Russia

Helen Arnold

RSVP
**RAINTREE
Steck-Vaughn**
P U B L I S H E R S
The Steck-Vaughn Company

Austin, Texas

Published by Raintree Steck-Vaughn Publishers, an imprint of Steck-Vaughn Company

A ZOË BOOK

Editor: Kath Davies, Helene Resky
Design: Jan Sterling, Sterling Associates
Map: Gecko Limited
Production: Grahame Griffiths

Library of Congress Cataloging-in-Publication Data

Arnold, Helen.
    Russia / Helen Arnold.
        p. cm. — (Postcards from)
    "A Zoë Book" — CIP p. 2.
    Includes index.
    ISBN 0-8172-4006-3 (lib. binding)
    ISBN 0-8172-4227-9 (softcover)
    1.Russia (Federation) — Description and travel — Juvenile literature.
    [1.Russia (Federation) — Description and travel.] I. Title. II. Series.
    DK510.28.A76 1996
    947–dc20   95–8100
                                                                   CIP
                                                                    AC

Printed and bound in the United States
  2 3 4 5 6 7 8 9 0 WZ 99 98 97

Photographic acknowledgments

The publishers wish to acknowledge, with thanks, the following photographic sources:

© Will & Dennis McIntyre / Tony Stone Images 28; The Hutchison Library / Stephen Seque - title page; Robert Harding Picture Library 8; Impact Photos / Simon Shepheard 12; / Alain Le Garsmeur 16; / Tony Page 26; David Williams Picture Library - cover bl, 20; Zefa - cover tl & r, 6, 10, 14, 18, 22, 24.

The publishers have made every effort to trace the copyright holders, but if they have inadvertently overlooked any, they will be pleased to make the necessary arrangement at the first opportunity.

Contents

All the words that appear in **bold** are explained in the Glossary on page 30.

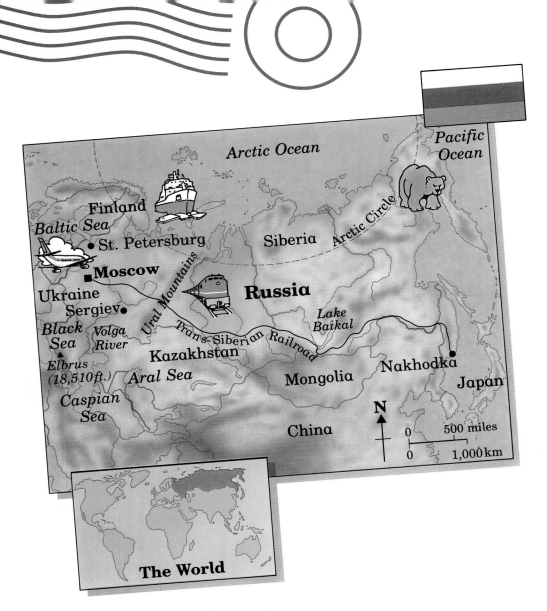

A big map of Russia
and a small map of the world

Dear Ian,

It took about nine hours to fly to Moscow from New York. It would take the same amount of time to fly across Russia. You can see Russia in red on the small map. It is the biggest country in the world.

Your cousin,

Craig

P.S. Dad says that Russia is twice as big as the United States, but fewer people live in Russia than in the United States.

The Kremlin, Red Square, Moscow

Dear Hayley,

Lots of **tourists** come to Red Square to see the Kremlin. It is in the middle of Moscow. Moscow is the **capital** city of Russia. Some people speak English here, but most people speak only Russian.

Your friend,

Amy

P.S. Russian writing looks strange. Mom says that the Russian alphabet is different from ours.

Shopping in Moscow at Christmas

Dear Josh,

Russian money is called *rubles*. Mom gave us some *rubles* to buy presents here. This is the largest indoor shopping center in Moscow. I am glad it is inside. The weather is very cold here.

Yours,

Joyce

P.S. Look at the difference between Russian and English writing. You can see the writing on the sign that says "Happy New Year."

9

Selling hot snacks on the street in
Moscow

Dear Tracey,

We buy hot snacks every day to keep warm! People sell all kinds of hot food on the streets in winter. The man in the picture is cooking *kabobs*, cubes of meat on a stick.

Love,

Anna

P.S. Mom says that each part of Russia has its own special dishes. There are soups, meat stews, and all kinds of fish. I tasted *caviar*. Dad says it's really fish eggs and very salty.

A *troika* ride in the snow

Dear Ben,

We went for a ride on a big sled like this one. It is called a *troika*. The horse pulled the sled very fast over the snow. I wore my new fur hat. It kept me really warm.

Yours,

Greg

P.S. Dad took us on the **subway**. It is called the *Metro*. It is the quickest way to travel across Moscow. The train was very crowded, but it was very clean.

The Summer Palace, St. Petersburg

Dear Ali,

St. Petersburg was the capital of Russia long ago. At that time there was a king, or *czar*, who ruled the country. Sometimes he lived in this huge palace. Now it is a **museum**.

Love,

Dawn

P.S. St. Petersburg is on the Neva River. We went on a boat trip to see some of the city. Mom says that the *czar* had a Winter Palace here, too. There are famous paintings in it.

An old Russian wooden house

Dear Harry,

Many old houses in Russia are made of wood. We saw houses like this one in the country. Most people in the cities live in new, **high-rise** apartments.

Your brother,

Andy

P.S. Dad says that some apartments are small and crowded. Grandparents often live with the rest of their family. Some families have small vacation homes in the country. They are called *dachas*.

Gorky Park, Moscow

Dear Scott,

This park has a fun fair for children on the holidays. I went on the Ferris wheel. I saw some people playing soccer. The Russians are good at many sports.

Love,

Eduardo

P.S. Mom says that Maxim Gorky was a famous writer. This park is named after him. The Russians play **chess** in the park.

On the Trans-Siberian Express train

Dear Becky,

You can see from the picture that this train has **bunks** for people as well as seats. This is because the train takes more than a week to cross Russia. It goes from Moscow in Europe to the Sea of Japan in Asia.

See you soon,

David

P.S. Dad says that the Trans-Siberian railroad line is more than 5,750 miles (9,250 km) long. It is the longest railroad line in the world.

Lake Baikal, Siberia

Dear Pete,

This is the deepest lake in the world. It is in Siberia, which is in the east of Russia. Siberia means "sleeping land." The weather here is very cold in winter. The lake freezes over.

Yours,

Lewis

P.S. My friend Boris says that more than 50 kinds of fish live in Lake Baikal. In the winter, people make holes in the ice to catch the fish. Bears and wolves live in the forests of Siberia.

Children give a show in the park on
May Day.

Dear Cindy,

The first day in May is a special day. Everyone in Russia has a holiday. Many people go to the parks, where there are **festivals**. They enjoy the warm spring weather. The long winter is over.

Love,

Joanna

P.S. My Dad says that the schools shut for three months in the summer. Some children go to summer camps.

A display of Russian dancing and the monastery at Sergiev

Dear Rob,

This building is a **monastery**. It was built about 700 years ago. The gold on the roofs is real! We saw Russian dancers on a stage like this one. The dancers wore special costumes.

Yours,

Ethan

P.S. Uncle Jake says that many Russians are **Christians**. Some churches have special paintings called *icons* inside them.

The Russian flag

Dear Darren,

A Russian flag like this one was flown more than 300 years ago. The *czars* ruled Russia at that time. The **communists** flew a red flag when they ruled Russia. Now Russia flies this flag again.

Love,

Mary

P.S. Mom says that about 80 years ago the *czar* was killed after a **revolution** in Russia. Then the communists ruled Russia. Now the Russian people choose their own leaders. Russia is a **democracy**.

Glossary

Bunk: A bed set on a wall. Sometimes two bunks are set, one above the other.

Capital: The town or city where people who rule the country meet

Chess: A board game for two people. The players take turns moving the chess pieces on the board.

Christians: People who follow the teachings of Jesus. Jesus lived about 2,000 years ago.

Communists: People who think that everything in a country should be owned and shared by all the people who live there

Democracy: A country where all the people choose the leaders they want to run the country

Festival: A time when people celebrate something special that happened in the past, or a special time of year

High-rise: Having many floors

Monastery: The buildings where monks live. Monks are men who have chosen a religious way of life.

Museum: A building where interesting things from the past are on display

P.S.: This stands for Post Script. A postscript is the part of a card or letter that is added at the end, after the person has signed it.

Revolution: A complete change in the way a country is ruled

Subway: A train that runs under the ground

Tourist: A person who is on vacation away from home

Index